BLAST OFF!
MERCURY

Helen and David Orme

ticktock

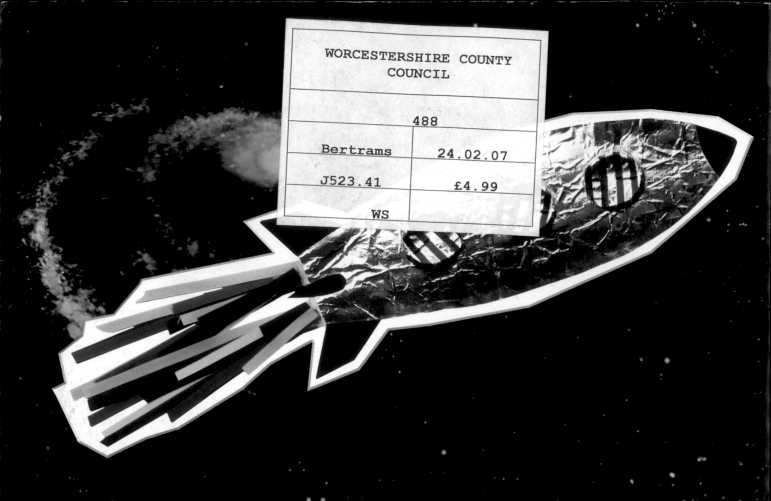

Copyright © ticktock Entertainment Ltd 2007
First published in Great Britain in 2006 by ticktock Media Ltd.,
Unit 2, Orchard Business Centre, North Farm Road,
Tunbridge Wells, Kent, TN2 3XF

ticktock project editor: Julia Adams
ticktock project designer: Emma Randall

We would like to thank: Sandra Voss, Tim Bones, James Powell,
Indexing Specialists (UK) Ltd.

ISBN 978 1 84696 049 9
Printed in China
A CIP catalogue record for this book is available from the British Library.

Picture credits
t=top, b=bottom, c=centre, l-left, r=right, bg=background
ESA: 23bl; NASA: front cover, 1tl, 6br, 8cr, 11brr, 18b, 19tr, 19bl, 21tl, 22cr, 23tr; Science Photo Library: 4/5bg (original), 9tl,
9bl, 10bl, 11tl; Shutterstock: 2/3bg, 6bl, 8cl, 9ctl, 9cbl, 13tr, 13bl, 24bg; ticktock picture archive: 1tr, 5tr, 7tl, 7br, 9cr, 11c, 12bl,
12br, 14bl, 14tr, 15tl, 15br, 16tr, 16bl, 17tr, 17bl, 20tr, 20cr, 20bl, 20br, 21br, 6/7bg, 10/11bg, 14/15bg, 18/19bg, 22/23bg
Every effort has been made to trace the copyright holders, and we apologise in advance for any unintentional omissions.
We would be pleased to insert the appropriate acknowledgements in any subsequent edition of this publication.

Contents

Where is Mercury? 4-5

Planet Facts 6-7

What's the Weather Like? 8-9

On the Surface 10-11

Ice on Mercury 12-13

Finding Mercury 14-15

What Can We See? 16-17

Missions to Mercury 18-19

Mercury Discoveries 20-21

Future Explorations 22-23

Glossary/Index 24

Where is Mercury?

There are eight planets in our solar system. The planets travel around the Sun. Mercury is the nearest planet to the Sun.

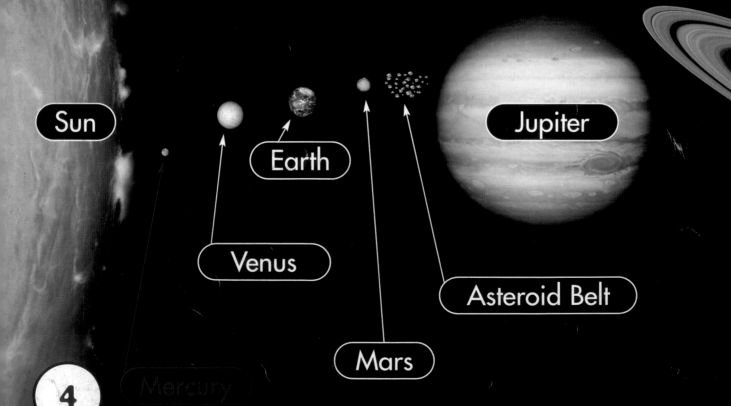

Sun

Earth

Venus

Mars

Mercury

Jupiter

Asteroid Belt

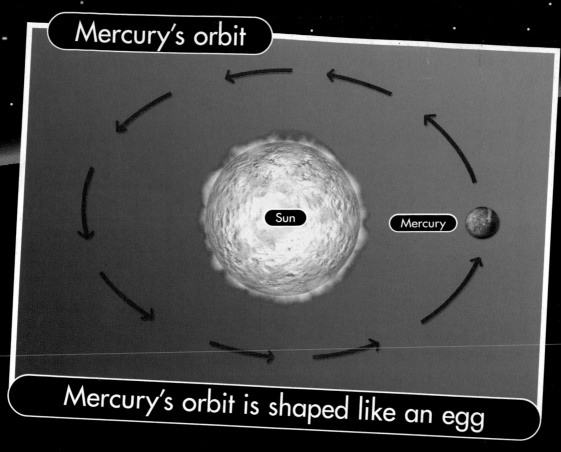

Mercury's orbit

Sun

Mercury

Mercury's orbit is shaped like an egg

Mercury travels round the Sun once every 88 **Earth days**. This journey is called its **orbit**. The time it takes for a planet to travel round the Sun once is called a **year**.

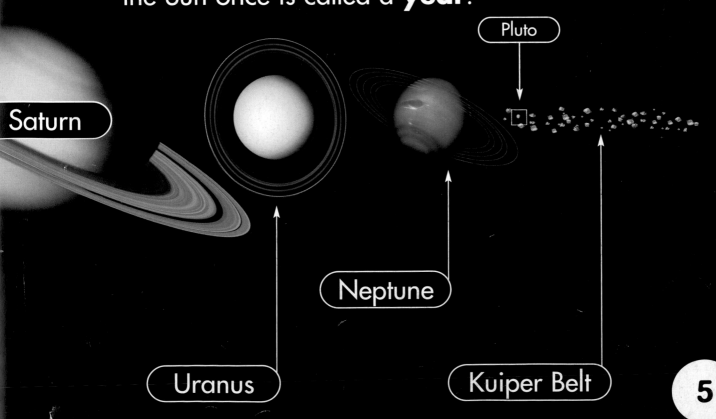

Pluto

Saturn

Neptune

Uranus

Kuiper Belt

Planet Facts

Mercury is a small, rocky planet. It is the smallest planet in our **solar system**. Mercury **orbits** the Sun faster than any other planet. It travels at 48 km a second!

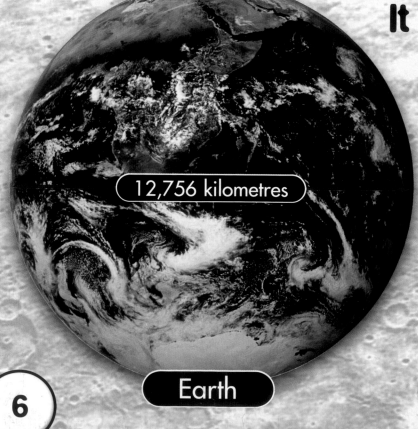

12,756 kilometres

Earth

4880 kilometres

Mercury

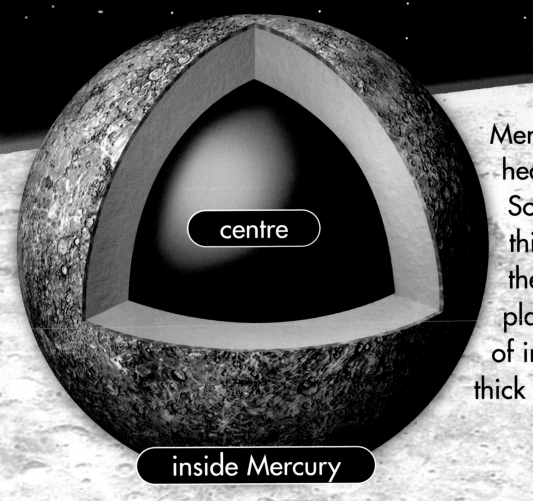

centre

inside Mercury

Mercury is a very heavy planet. Scientists think this is because the centre of the planet is made of iron. It is very thick and heavy.

A planet is always spinning around.

The time it takes for a planet to spin around once is called a day. Mercury's day is the same length as 59 **Earth days!**

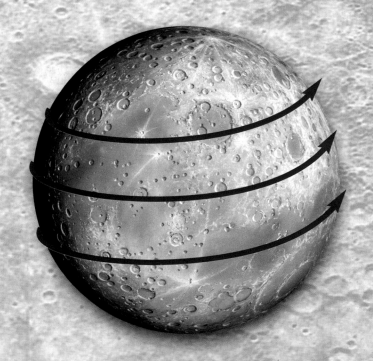

What's the Weather Like?

Mercury is the closest planet to the Sun. That is why it is one of the hottest planets.

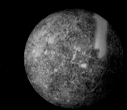

IMAGINE...

During the day it is hot enough on Mercury to melt lead!

8

This is a thermometer showing the temperatures on Mercury. You can compare them to the ones we have here on Earth!

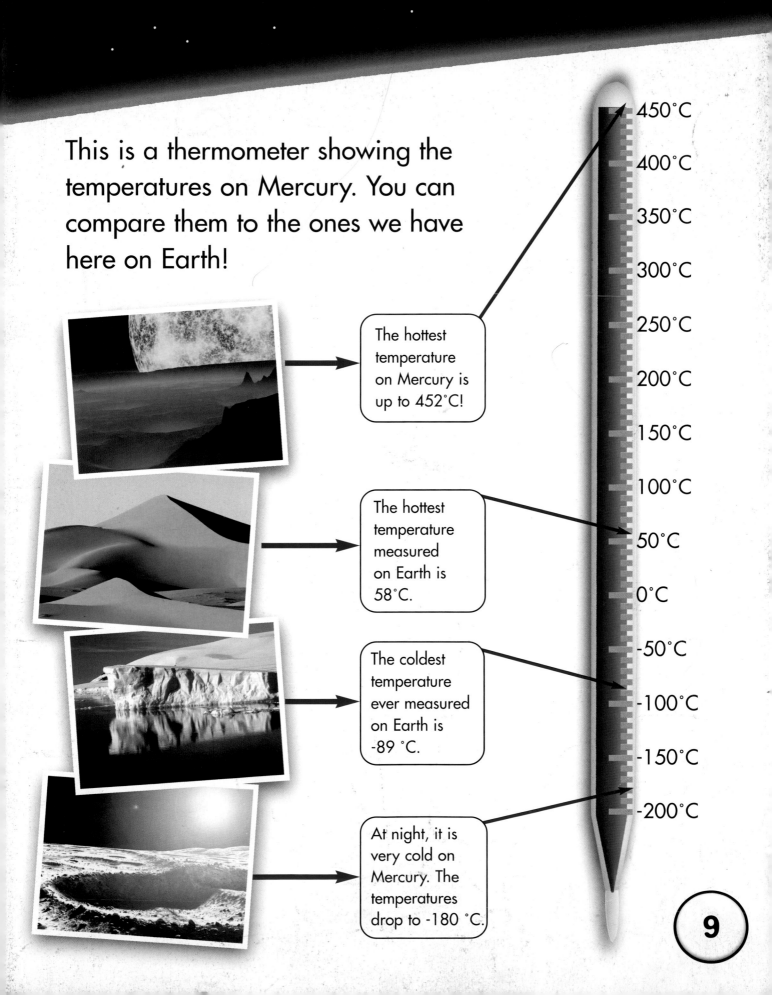

The hottest temperature on Mercury is up to 452°C!

The hottest temperature measured on Earth is 58°C.

The coldest temperature ever measured on Earth is -89 °C.

At night, it is very cold on Mercury. The temperatures drop to -180 °C.

450°C
400°C
350°C
300°C
250°C
200°C
150°C
100°C
50°C
0°C
-50°C
-100°C
-150°C
-200°C

On the Surface

The surface of Mercury has huge cliffs and cracks. They are hundreds of kilometres long and up to 3 km high! The cliffs were probably made millions of years ago.

3 kilometres

Mercury was very, very hot when it was a new planet. The huge cracks formed across the surface when Mercury cooled down.

Mercury also has one of the largest basins in the **solar system**. It measures about 1,350 km across!

The Caloris Basin was created by a huge rock hitting the surface of Mercury. Vibrations went right through Mercury and cracked the surface on the other side!

This is a photograph of half of the Caloris Basin.

Ice on Mercury

In 1991, scientists thought they found ice at Mercury's North Pole. This is very important because ice is frozen water. Life is only possible with water. This is why scientists always look for water on planets.

Mercury's North Pole

This is the Arecibo radio telescope in Puerto Rico. Scientists used it to look for ice on Mercury. It is one of the largest telescopes in the world.

At Mercury's North Pole there are places where the Sun's heat never reaches, so the ice would never melt. These places may be in the shadow of cliffs or at the bottom of **craters**.

crater

comet

The ice may have come from deep inside Mercury. It may also have come from **comets**, that have crashed into its surface.

13

Finding Mercury

For thousands of years,
people have studied the sky.
In the beginning, they didn't even
have telescopes.

We can see Mercury
without a telescope
in the morning...

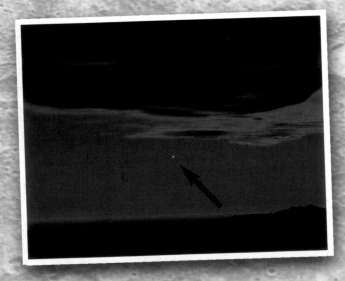

...and the evening.

The ancient Greeks knew that it was one planet,
but they still gave it two names. They called it
Apollo in the morning and Hermes in the evening.

Mercury

The ancient Romans gave the planet the name Mercury. They named the fast moving planet after Mercury, their god of travel.

This telescope was invented by the English scientist Isaac Newton in 1668. Scientists using the telescope were able to see and study Mercury much more easily.

What Can We See?

The best time to see Mercury is in the early morning and as it gets dark at night.

For the best view of Mercury, you should use a small telescope after the Sun has set.

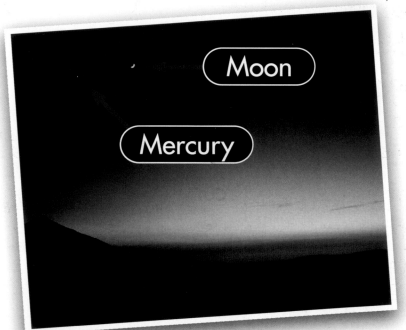

Moon

Mercury

Mercury is easier to see if you live in the southern half of the world.

16

Mercury is difficult to see from the Earth. This is because we have to look towards the Sun to see it. But the Sun is huge compared to Mercury. Looking at the Sun is also very dangerous.

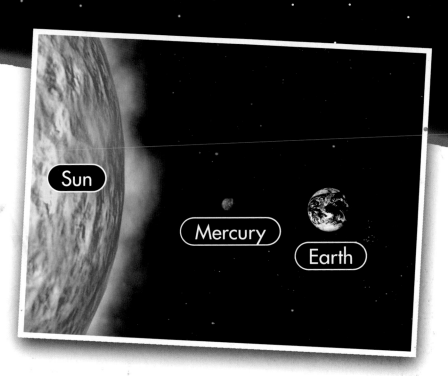

Sun

Mercury

Earth

Astronomers study Mercury when it moves in front of the Sun with special telescopes. This happens about 13 times in a century.

Mercury

Sun

Mercury looks like a tiny black dot against the Sun.

Missions to Mercury

It is difficult to send a **space probe** to Mercury. This is because it is so close to the Sun. Unless scientists are very careful, the spacecraft would be burnt up by the Sun!

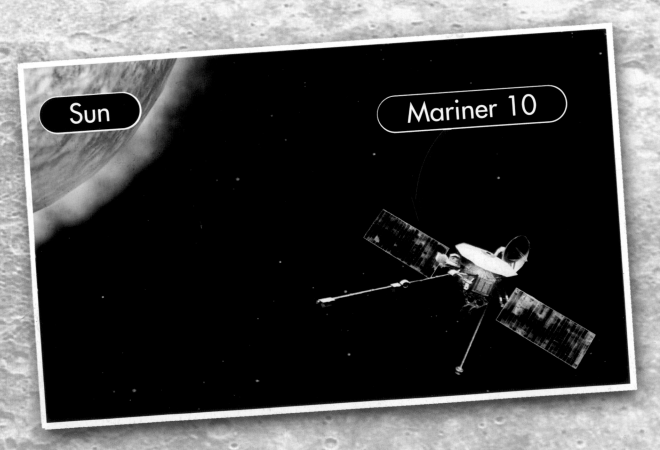

Sun

Mariner 10

Mariner 10 is the only space probe to have reached Mercury. It arrived there in 1974 and flew by the planet 3 times.

Mariner 10 managed three close fly-bys of the planet. It was able to photograph almost half of Mercury's surface. It also sent back information about the temperatures on Mercury.

45 km

Mariner 10 also took pictures showing more detail of the surface. This photo is of a huge **crater** on Mercury. It is called the Degas Crater. It is 45 km wide!

Space probes

are not the only way we can find out about planets. We can use telescopes based right here on Earth.

Some telescopes let us see farther than others. The small photos on this page show how well Mercury can be seen from different telescopes.

home telescope

scientist's telescope

This is a picture of Mercury taken by a **radio telescope.**

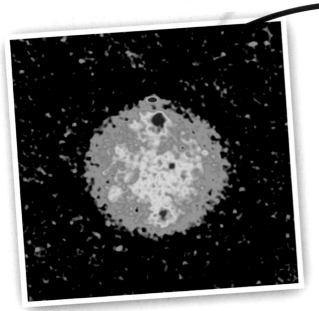

Mercury's North Pole

The different colours tell scientists about the temperature of the surface of the planet. The top red area is the North Pole where scientists think they have found ice.

radio telescope

21

MESSENGER

(short for **MErcury Surface, Space ENvironment, GEochemistry and Ranging mission**) was launched by **NASA** in August 2004. It is the second mission to Mercury.

MESSENGER should fly past Mercury in 2008 and 2009. In 2011 it will go into **orbit** around the planet.

MESSENGER will photograph the surface of the whole planet. It will send back much more information about the atmosphere and what Mercury is made of.

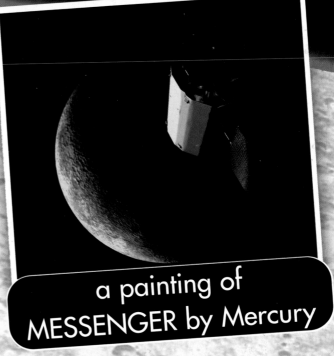

a painting of MESSENGER by Mercury

a painting of Bepi-Colombo by Mercury

European and Japanese scientists have planned a mission to Mercury for 2013. It will be called Bepi-Colombo. This should reach Mercury in 2019. It will help make a very exact map of Mercury.

Glossary

Asteroid A rocky object that orbits the Sun. Most asteroids orbit the Sun between Mars and Jupiter.

Astronomers People who study space and the objects found in space.

Comets Objects usually made of ice and frozen gas that are in orbit around the Sun.

Crater A hole in the surface of a planet or a moon. It is made either by a volcano or when a rock from space crashes into the surface and leaves a deep dent.

Earth day A day is the time it takes a planet to spin around once. A day on Earth is 24 hours long.

Lead A heavy grey metal. It melts at about 327°C.

NASA (Short for National Aeronautics and Space Administration) A group of scientists and astronauts who research space.

Orbit The path planets or other objects take around the Sun, or satellites take around planets.

Radio telescope A tool to help find out about the surface of a planet that is very far away. The radio

telescope works out the temperatures and surface of a planet with the help of special signals called radio waves.

Solar system The Sun and everything that is in orbit around it.

Space probe A spacecraft sent from Earth to explore the solar system.

Sunspots Areas in the Sun's surface that are slightly cooler and darker than other ares.

Year The time it takes a planet to orbit the Sun.

Index

ancient Greeks/Romans 14

astronomers 17

atmosphere 23

basins 11

comets 13

craters 13, 19

Earth 6, 9

Earth days 5, 7

ice 12

iron 7

lead 8

MESSENGER 22–23

missions 18–19

NASA 22

North Pole of Mercury 12–13, 21

orbits 5, 6, 22

planets 4–5

scientists 7, 12, 18

solar system 6, 11

space probes 18, 20

Sun 4–6, 8, 17

surface of Mercury 10, 19, 21, 23

telescopes 12, 14–17, 20–21

weather 8–9

years 5